MATH FOR MINECRAFTERS

ADVENTURES IN ADDITION & SUBTRACTION

VOLUME 2

Level Up Your Skills with New Practice Problems and Activities!

Sky Pony Press
New York

Copyright © 2021 by Hollan Publishing, Inc.
Minecraft® is a registered trademark of Notch Development AB.

The Minecraft game is copyright © Mojang AB.

Sky Pony Press books may be purchased in bulk at special discounts for sales promotion, corporate gifts, fund-raising, or educational purposes. Special editions can also be created to specifications. For details, contact the Special Sales Department, Sky Pony Press, 307 West 36th Street, 11th Floor, New York, NY 10018 or info@skyhorsepublishing.com.

Sky Pony® is a registered trademark of Skyhorse Publishing, Inc.®, a Delaware corporation.

Minecraft® is a registered trademark of Notch Development AB. The Minecraft game is copyright © Mojang AB.

Visit our website at www.skyponypress.com.

10 9 8 7 6 5 4 3 2 1

Library of Congress Cataloging-in-Publication Data is available on file.

Print ISBN: 978-1-5107-6621-1

Cover design by Brian Peterson
Interior design by Noora Cox
Cover and interior illustrations by Amanda Brack

Printed in China

A NOTE TO PARENTS

When you want to reinforce classroom skills at home, it's crucial to have kid-friendly learning materials. This *Math for Minecrafters: Adventures in Addition & Subtraction, Volume 2* workbook transforms math practice into an irresistible adventure complete with diamond armor, zombie pigmen, ghasts, and skeletons. That means less arguing over homework and more fun overall.

Math for Minecrafters: Adventures in Addition & Subtraction, Volume 2 is also fully aligned with National Common Core Standards for 1st and 2nd grade math. What does that mean, exactly? All of the problems in this book correspond to what your child is expected to learn in school. This eliminates confusion and builds confidence for greater homework-time success!

The primary focus of this Volume 2 workbook is math facts repetition and fluency. With enough supplemental practice, your child will commit the answers to common addition and subtraction problems to memory and level up their math ability.

As the workbook progresses, the math problems become more advanced. Encourage your child to progress at his or her own pace. Learning is best when students are challenged, but not frustrated. What's most important is that your Minecrafter is engaged in his or her own learning.

Whether it's the joy of seeing their favorite game characters on every page or the thrill of solving challenging problems just like Steve and Alex, there is something in this workbook to entice even the most reluctant math student.

Happy adventuring!

ADDITION BY GROUPING

Circle the groups of 2. Then count on and write the total. The first one is done for you.

1.    Answer: 5

2.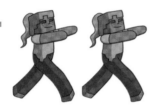

Answer: _____

3.

Answer: _____

4.

Answer: _____

5.

Answer: _____

MYSTERY MESSAGE
WITH ADDITION AND SUBTRACTION

Add or subtract. Then use the letters to fill in the blanks below and reveal the answer to Alex's joke.

1. 10 - 2 = _____ C

2. 4 + 3 = _____ F

3. 15 - 10 = _____ I

4. 6 + 4 = _____ R

5. 7 + 7 = _____ E

6. 13 - 9 = _____ T

7. 9 + 3 = _____ N

8. 8 - 5 = _____ M

9. 7 + 8 = _____ A

Q: What word could also mean "digging up art"?

Copy the letters from the answers above to solve the joke.

_____

3   5   12   14   8   10   15   7   4

ADDITION IN BASE 10

Add the numbers.

1. $2 + 3 = $ _____

2. $4 + 1 = $ _____

3. $3 + 4 = $ _____

4. $0 + 5 = $ _____

5. $7 + 1 = $ _____

6. $5 + 2 = $ _____

7. $1 + 6 = $ _____

8. $4 + 4 = $ _____

9. $9 + 1 = $ _____

10. $6 + 4 = $ _____

SKIP COUNT CHALLENGE

Count by 2s and fill in the empty spaces to help Alex tame her pig.

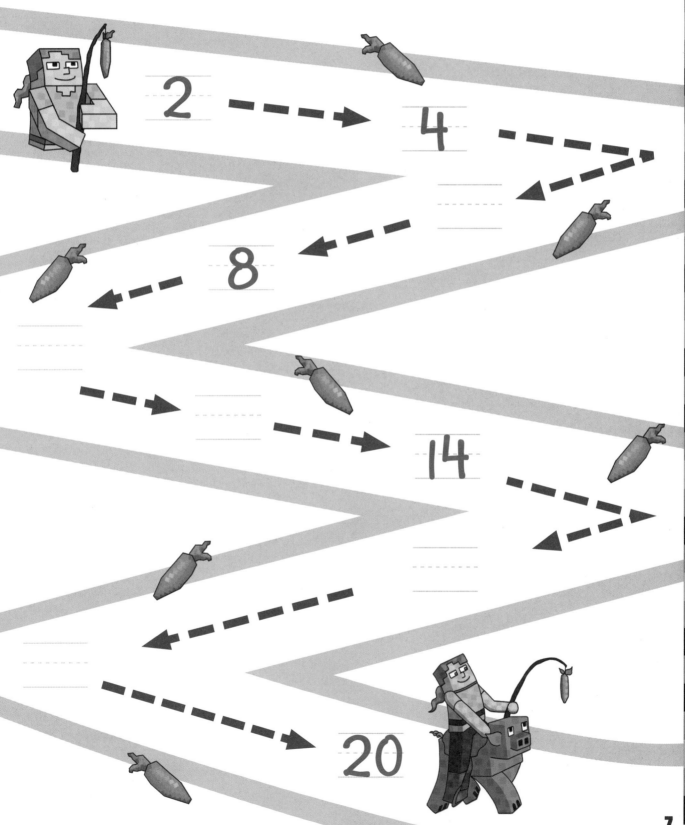

ADDITION MYSTERY NUMBER

There is a number hidden behind these gold ingots. Count on to find the mystery number. The first one is done for you.

1.

$$\begin{array}{r} 4 \\ + \\ \hline 6 \end{array}$$

= **2**

2.

$$\begin{array}{r} 3 \\ + \\ \hline 8 \end{array}$$

= _____

3.

$$\begin{array}{r} 7 \\ + \\ \hline 9 \end{array}$$

= _____

4.

$$\begin{array}{r} 2 \\ + \\ \hline 5 \end{array}$$

= _____

5.

$$\begin{array}{r} 4 \\ + \\ \hline 4 \end{array}$$

= _____

6.

$$\begin{array}{r} 3 \\ + \\ \hline 7 \end{array}$$

= _____

SUBTRACTION MYSTERY NUMBER

There is a number hidden behind these glowstone blocks. Subtract to find the mystery number. The first one is done for you.

1.

$$8 - \blacksquare = 6$$

$\blacksquare = 2$

2.

$$7 - \blacksquare = 4$$

$\blacksquare = $ _____

3.

$$2 - \blacksquare = 0$$

$\blacksquare = $ _____

4.

$$8 - \blacksquare = 5$$

$\blacksquare = $ _____

5.

$$5 - \blacksquare = 1$$

$\blacksquare = $ _____

6.

$$9 - \blacksquare = 8$$

$\blacksquare = $ _____

ADDITION IN BASE 10

Add the numbers. Then write the answer using tally marks. The first one is done for you.

1. 2 + 2 =   4   **TALLY** ||||

2. 3 + 4 =   _____   **TALLY**

3. 1 + 5 =   _____   **TALLY**

4. 3 + 2 =   _____   **TALLY**

5. 2 + 1 =   _____   **TALLY**

6. 4 + 4 =   _____   **TALLY**

SUBTRACTION IN BASE 10

Subtract the numbers. Then write the answer using tally marks. The first one is done for you.

1. 6 - 3 =   3   **TALLY**
   |||

2. 5 - 1 =   **TALLY**

3. 7 - 2 =   **TALLY**

4. 6 - 5 =   **TALLY**

5. 9 - 3 =   **TALLY**

6. 10 - 3 =   **TALLY**

ADDITION BY GROUPING

Circle the groups of 3. Then count on and write the total. The first one is done for you.

1.

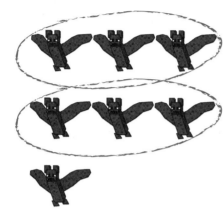

Answer: 7

2.

Answer: _____

3.

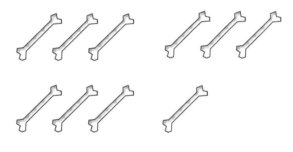

Answer: _____

4.

Answer: _____

5.

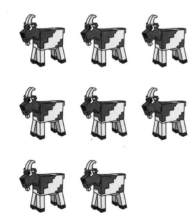

Answer: _____

6.

Answer: _____

MYSTERY MESSAGE
WITH ADDITION AND SUBTRACTION

Add or subtract. Then use the letters to fill in the blanks below and reveal the answer to Alex's joke.

1. 7 - 2 = _____ **S**   2. 4 + 3 = _____ **E**

3. 9 - 6 = _____ **N**   4. 6 + 3 = _____ **T**

5. 8 + 0 = _____ **L**   6. 9 - 8 = _____ **O**

7. 9 - 3 = _____ **K**   8. 10 - 8 = _____ **A**

Q: What has bones, but not flesh, and a face but no skin?

Copy the letters from the answers above to solve the riddle.

_____ _____ _____ _____ _____ _____ _____ _____ _____

2   5   6   7   8   7   9   1   3

PUFFER FISH'S GUIDE TO PLACE VALUE

Identify the number that belongs in the place-value chart and write it there. The first one is done for you.

1.  52

TENS
5

2.  73

ONES

3.  25

ONES

4.  62

TENS

5.  21

ONES

6.  30

ONES

7.  42

TENS

8.  94

TENS

SKIP COUNT CHALLENGE

Count by 3s and fill in the empty spaces to help Alex build a giant beacon pyramid.

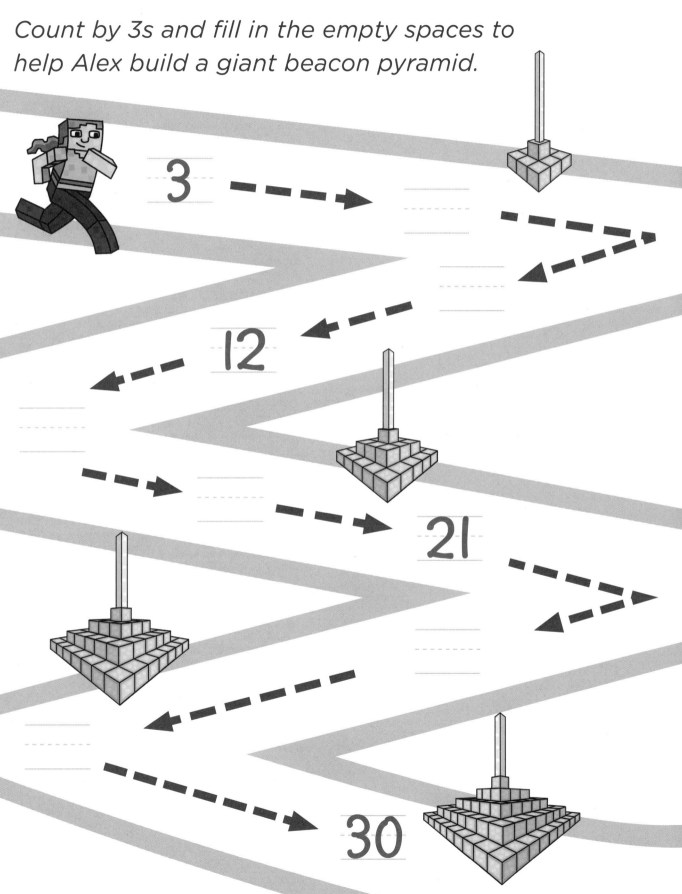

3

12

21

30

ADDITION AND SUBTRACTION MYSTERY NUMBER

There is a number hidden behind these cobblestone blocks. Add or subtract to find the mystery number. The first one is done for you.

1.

$$\begin{array}{r} 7 \\ + \; \blacksquare \\ \hline 10 \end{array}$$

2.

$$\begin{array}{r} 8 \\ - \; \blacksquare \\ \hline 2 \end{array}$$

3.

$$\begin{array}{r} 5 \\ + \; \blacksquare \\ \hline 10 \end{array}$$

4.

$$\begin{array}{r} 9 \\ - \; \blacksquare \\ \hline 9 \end{array}$$

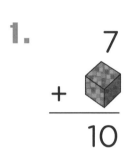 = **3**

◼ = _____

◼ = _____

◼ = _____

5.

$$\begin{array}{r} 4 \\ + \; \blacksquare \\ \hline 8 \end{array}$$

6.

$$\begin{array}{r} 2 \\ + \; \blacksquare \\ \hline 9 \end{array}$$

7.

$$\begin{array}{r} 8 \\ - \; \blacksquare \\ \hline 0 \end{array}$$

8.

$$\begin{array}{r} 3 \\ + \; \blacksquare \\ \hline 9 \end{array}$$

◼ = _____

◼ = _____

◼ = _____

◼ = _____

MYSTERY MESSAGE

Use the chart to solve the riddle.

3	E
4	R
5	E
6	C
7	R
9	P
10	G
11	E

Q: What's green and black and spawns all over?

6 7 11 11 9 3 4

3 10 10

ADDITION IN BASE 10

Add the numbers.

1. 2 + 8 = _____

2. 4 + 6 = _____

3. 3 + 7 = _____

4. 5 + 5 = _____

5. 7 + 3 = _____

6. 6 + 4 = _____

7. 9 + 1 = _____

8. 4 + 6 = _____

9. 1 + 9 = _____

10. 8 + 2 = _____

SUBTRACTION IN BASE 10

Subtract the numbers.

1. 10 - 8 = _____

2. 10 - 6 = _____

3. 10 - 7 = _____

4. 10 - 5 = _____

5. 10 - 3 = _____

6. 10 - 4 = _____

7. 10 - 1 = _____

8. 10 - 0 = _____

9. 10 - 9 = _____

10. 10 - 2 = _____

ADDITION MATH FACTS WITH 0 AND 1

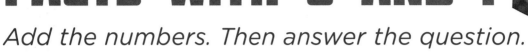

Add the numbers. Then answer the question.

1. 1 + 0 =

2. 1 + 1 =

3. 2 + 0 =

4. 2 + 1 =

5. 3 + 0 =

6. 3 + 1 =

7. 4 + 0 =

8. 4 + 1 =

9. 5 + 0 =

10. 5 + 1 =

11. 6 + 0 =

12. 6 + 1 =

13. 7 + 0 =

14. 7 + 1 =

15. 8 + 0 =

16. 8 + 1 =

17. 9 + 0 =

18. 9 + 1 =

19. 10 + 0 =

20. 10 + 1 =

ADDITION MATH FACTS WITH 2 AND 3

Add the numbers.

1. $1 + 2 =$ _____

2. $1 + 3 =$ _____

3. $2 + 2 =$ _____

4. $2 + 3 =$ _____

5. $3 + 2 =$ _____

6. $3 + 3 =$ _____

7. $4 + 2 =$ _____

8. $4 + 3 =$ _____

9. $5 + 2 =$ _____

10. $5 + 3 =$ _____

11. $6 + 2 =$ _____

12. $6 + 3 =$ _____

13. $7 + 2 =$ _____

14. $7 + 3 =$ _____

15. $8 + 2 =$ _____

16. $3 + 6 =$ _____

17. $5 + 2 =$ _____

18. $4 + 3 =$ _____

19. $0 + 2 =$ _____

20. $0 + 3 =$ _____

SKELETON'S GUIDE TO PLACE VALUE

Use the number on each skeleton to fill in the place-value chart.

Example:

Tens	Ones
3	2

1.

Tens	Ones

2.

Tens	Ones

3.

Tens	Ones

4.

Tens	Ones

5.

Tens	Ones

6.

Tens	Ones

SKIP COUNT CHALLENGE

Count by 4s and fill in the empty spaces to help Steve craft his diamond armor.

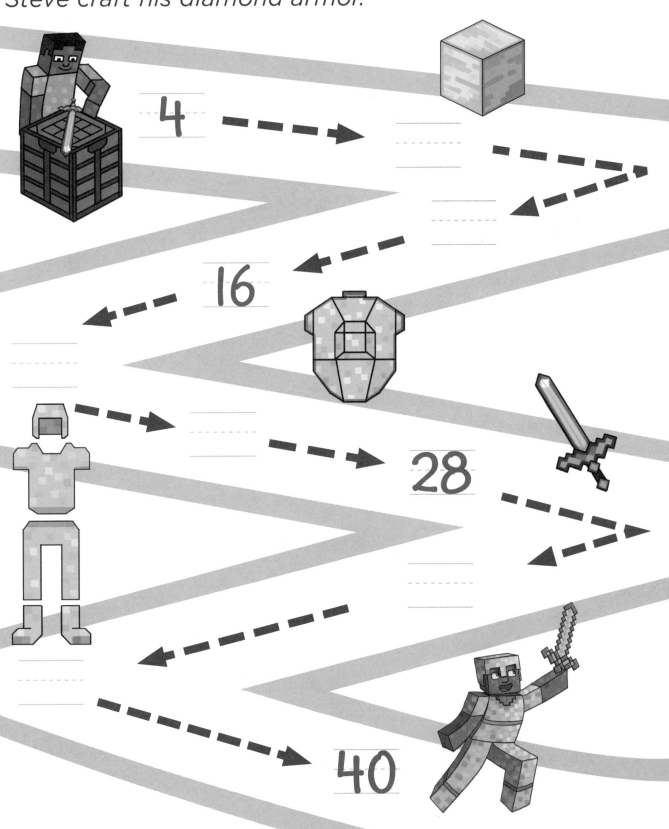

4

16

28

40

WORD PROBLEMS WITH ADDITION

Read the word problems. Use addition to help you find the answer. The first one is done for you.

1. You have 3 wooden planks to make a crafting table and your friend gives you 1 more. How many wooden planks do you have?

$$3 + 1 = 4$$

Answer: **4 wooden planks**

2. Steve crafts 3 iron swords at his crafting table. The next day, he crafts 4 more iron swords. How many iron swords does Steve craft? Fill in what you know in the boxes so you can find the answer.

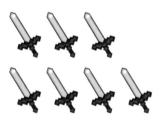

_____ + _____ = _____

Answer: _____

3. Alex has 4 carrots to tame her pig and Steve gives her 4 more. How many carrots does Alex have?

_____ + _____ = _____

Answer: _____

4. Steve grows 4 melons in his garden and Alex grows 2 melons in her garden. How many melons do they have all together?

_____ + _____ = _____

Answer: _____

WORD PROBLEMS WITH SUBTRACTION

Read the word problems. Use subtraction to help you find the answer. The first one is done for you.

1. You have 8 diamond blocks and use 3 to craft a helmet. How many diamond blocks do you have left?

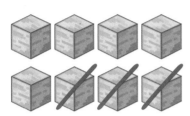

$$8 - 3 = 5$$

Answer: 5 diamond blocks

2. Alex has 10 TNT blocks. She uses 5 TNT blocks to blow up a mob's hiding place. How many blocks does she have left?

____ - ____ = ____

Answer: ____

3. Steve adds 5 shulker spawn eggs to his inventory. Later that day, he uses 3 of them. How many shulker spawn eggs are in his inventory?

____ - ____ = ____

Answer: ____

4. Alex crafts 8 wooden swords in the morning. In the afternoon, she breaks 3 of them fighting zombies. How many wooden swords does Alex have left?

____ - ____ = ____

Answer: ____

ADDITION IN BASE 10

Add the numbers. Then answer the questions.

1. 4 + 2 = _____

2. 2 + 5 = _____

3. 6 + 3 = _____

4. 4 + 1 = _____

5. 8 + 1 = _____

6. 4 + 6 = _____

7. 2 + 5 = _____

8. 6 + 2 = _____

Q: Circle the answers that are even. What do you notice when you add an even number to an even number?

A: _____

Q: Circle the answers that are odd. What do you notice when you add an even number to an odd number?

A: _____

ADDITION IN BASE 10

Add the numbers. Then answer the questions.

1. 8 - 2 = _____

2. 10 - 6 = _____

3. 9 - 2 = _____

4. 7 - 4 = _____

5. 8 - 4 = _____

6. 7 - 6 = _____

7. 9 - 4 = _____

8. 10 - 8 = _____

Q: Circle the answers that are even. What do you notice when you subtract an even number from an even number?

A: _____

Q: Circle the answers that are odd. What do you notice when you subtract an even number from an odd number?

A: _____

ADDITION MATH FACTS WITH 4 AND 5

Add the numbers.

1. 1 + 4 =

2. 1 + 5 =

3. 2 + 4 =

4. 2 + 5 =

5. 3 + 4 =

6. 3 + 5 =

7. 4 + 4 =

8. 4 + 5 =

9. 5 + 4 =

10. 5 + 5 =

11. 6 + 4 =

12. 6 + 5 =

13. 7 + 4 =

14. 7 + 5 =

15. 8 + 4 =

16. 8 + 5 =

17. 9 + 4 =

18. 9 + 5 =

19. 10 + 4 =

20. 10 + 5 =

PROPERTIES OF ADDITION

A sneaky witch swapped the order of the numbers in the equations below. Switch the numbers back and solve both equations.

Example: 1 + 2 = 3

2 + 1 = 3

1. 3 + 4 =

2. 5 + 3 =

3. 7 + 2 =

4. 8 + 1 =

5. 4 + 5 =

6. 10 + 0 =

What do you notice about the answers in each pair?

MOOSHROOM'S GUIDE TO PLACE VALUE

Identify the number that belongs in the place-value chart and write it there. The first one is done for you.

1.  392

TENS

9

2.  874

HUNDREDS

3.  705

ONES

4.  304

TENS

5. 297

HUNDREDS

6.  430

ONES

7.  865

TENS

8.  329

HUNDREDS

SKIP COUNT CHALLENGE

Count by 5s and fill in the empty spaces to help the arctic fox get to the snowy Taiga biome before the wolf catches it.

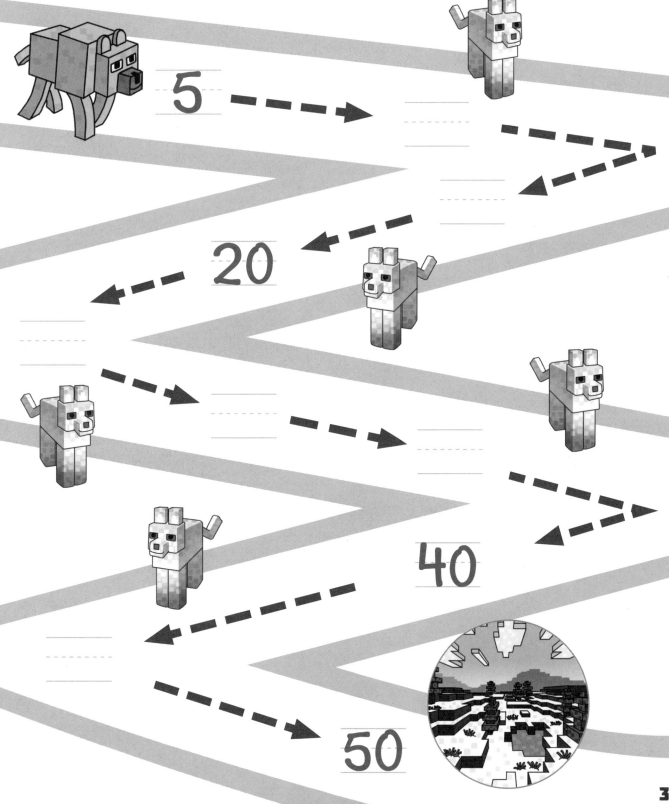

5

20

40

50

WORD PROBLEMS WITH ADDITION

Read the word problems. Use addition to help you find the answer. The first one is done for you.

1. You have 3 diamond blocks. You mine 4 more diamond blocks. How many diamond blocks do you have?

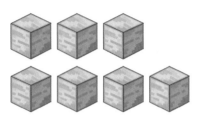

$$3 + 4 = 7$$

Answer: 7 diamond blocks

2. Alex has 4 torches to light her way. She finds 7 more torches in a stronghold. How many torches does Alex have?

____ + ____ = ____

Answer: ____

3. Alex has 3 plants. Steve gives her 7 more. How many plants does she have now?

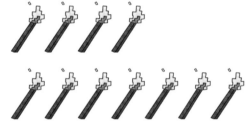

____ + ____ = ____

Answer: ____

4. Alex finds a field of red mushrooms. She collects 6 mushrooms one day and 6 mushrooms the next day. How many mushrooms does Alex collect?

____ + ____ = ____

Answer: ____

WORD PROBLEMS WITH SUBTRACTION

Read the word problems. Use subtraction to help you find the answer. The first one is done for you.

1. There are 9 tools in your inventory. You use 6 of them. How many tools do you have left?

$$9 - 6 = 3$$

Answer: **3 tools**

2. Steve grows 12 sugar cane plants in his garden. He uses 7 of the plants to make paper. How many plants does Steve have left?

_____ - _____ = _____

Answer: _____

3. Alex has 12 horses on her farm. She put saddles on 4 of them. How many horses do not have saddles?

_____ - _____ = _____

Answer: _____

4. Steve crafts 10 pumpkin pies. He eats 3 of them. How many pies are left?

_____ - _____ = _____

Answer: _____

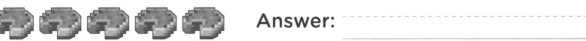

ADDITION AND PLACE VALUE

Add the numbers. Then write the values in the boxes. The first one is done for you.

1. 9 + 6 =   15

Tens	Ones
1	5

2. 10 + 2 =

Tens	Ones

3. 8 + 6 =

Tens	Ones

4. 17 + 3 =

Tens	Ones

5. 8 + 5 =

Tens	Ones

6. 11 + 9 =

Tens	Ones

SUBTRACTION AND PLACE VALUE

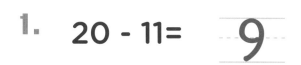

Subtract the numbers. Then write the values in the boxes. The first one is done for you.

1. **20 - 11 =** 9

Tens	Ones
0	9

2. **18 - 12 =**

Tens	Ones

3. **17 - 7 =**

Tens	Ones

4. **11 - 4 =**

Tens	Ones

5. **20 - 4 =**

Tens	Ones

6. **13 - 13 =**

Tens	Ones

SUBTRACTION MATH FACTS FROM 0 TO 10

Subtract the numbers.

1. $10 - 2 =$

2. $7 - 3 =$

3. $10 - 6 =$

4. $6 - 3 =$

5. $6 - 6 =$

6. $10 - 4 =$

7. $8 - 4 =$

8. $10 - 3 =$

9. $7 - 4 =$

10. $5 - 4 =$

11. $9 - 4 =$

12. $10 - 5 =$

13. $3 - 1 =$

14. $8 - 3 =$

15. $6 - 2 =$

16. $7 - 5 =$

17. $9 - 2 =$

18. $10 - 7 =$

19. $6 - 1 =$

20. $6 - 4 =$

SUBTRACTION MATH FACTS FROM 0 TO 10

Subtract the numbers.

1. 10 - 4 = _____

2. 7 - 4 = _____

3. 8 - 3 = _____

4. 6 - 3 = _____

5. 6 - 5 = _____

6. 9 - 1 = _____

7. 9 - 5 = _____

8. 7 - 5 = _____

9. 10 - 3 = _____

10. 10 - 7 = _____

11. 9 - 6 = _____

12. 9 - 1 = _____

13. 5 - 1 = _____

14. 6 - 4 = _____

15. 8 - 4 = _____

16. 7 - 3 = _____

17. 8 - 2 = _____

18. 10 - 2 = _____

19. 10 - 6 = _____

20. 9 - 4 = _____

LLAMA'S GUIDE TO PLACE VALUE

Use the number on the llama to fill in the place value chart.

Example:

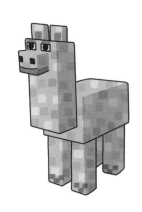

Hundreds	
2	
Tens	**Ones**
3	8

1.

Hundreds	
Tens	**Ones**

2.

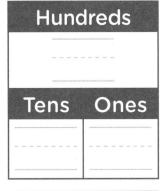

Hundreds	
Tens	**Ones**

3.

Hundreds	
Tens	**Ones**

4.

Hundreds	
Tens	**Ones**

5.

Hundreds	
Tens	**Ones**

6.

Hundreds	
Tens	**Ones**

SKIP COUNT CHALLENGE

Count by 6s and fill in the empty spaces to help Steve escape the zombie.

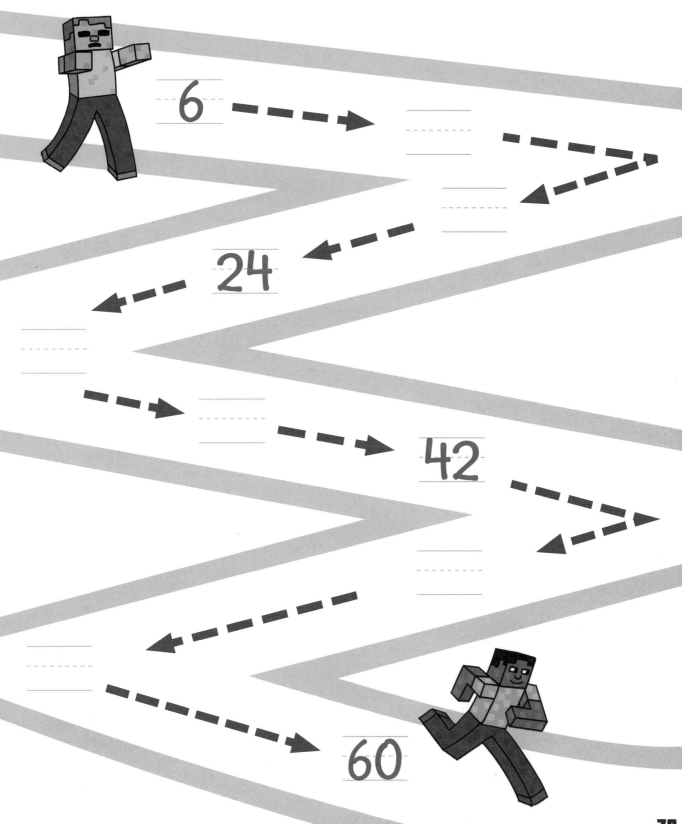

6

24

42

60

ADDITION MYSTERY NUMBER

There is a number hidden behind these lava blocks. Count on to find the mystery number.

1.

8
+
———
13

 = _____

2.

6
+
———
13

= _____

3.

4
+
———
12

= _____

4.

5
+
———
15

= _____

5.

6
+
———
20

= _____

6.

8
+
———
14

= _____

7.

2
+
———
8

= _____

8.

5
+
———
20

= _____

9.

9
+
———
18

= _____

MYSTERY MESSAGE WITH ADDITION

Add the answers from page 40 to the chart.
Then use the chart to solve the riddle.

QUESTION	ANSWER	LETTER
1.		N
2.		B
3.		K
4.		E
5.		Y
6.		I
7.		U
8.		R
9.		L

Q: What's cute and cuddly and fuzzy and deadly?
Copy the letters from the chart to solve the riddle.

8   14   9   9   10   15

7   6   5   5   14

EXPANDED FORM IN BASE 10

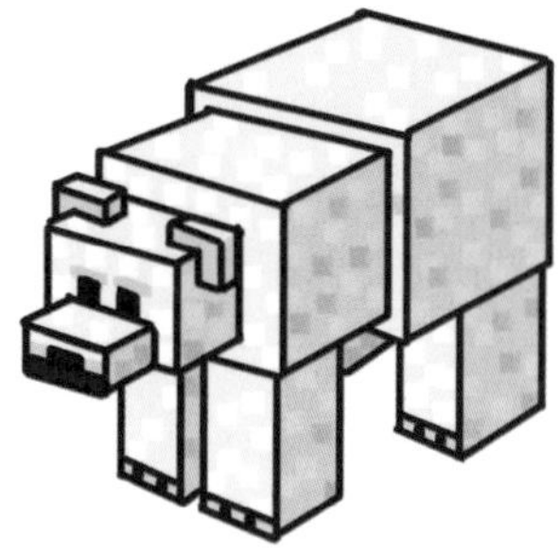

Write the number on each polar bear in expanded form in the space provided.

Example:

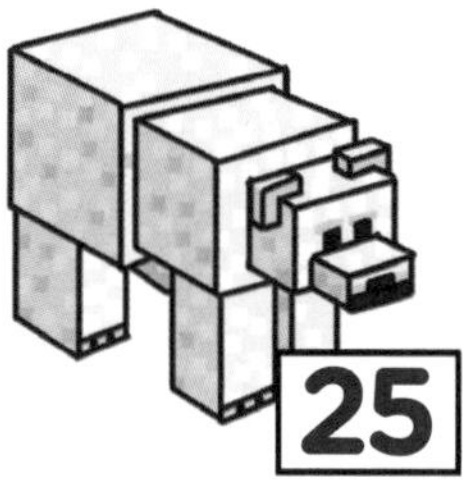

20 + 5

1.

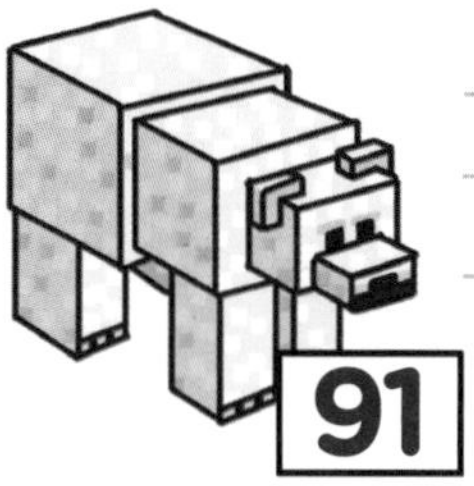

2.

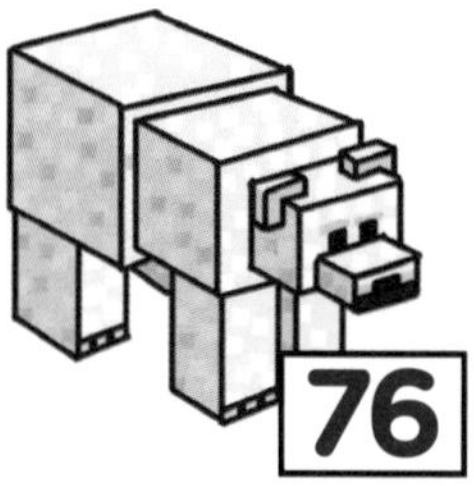

3.

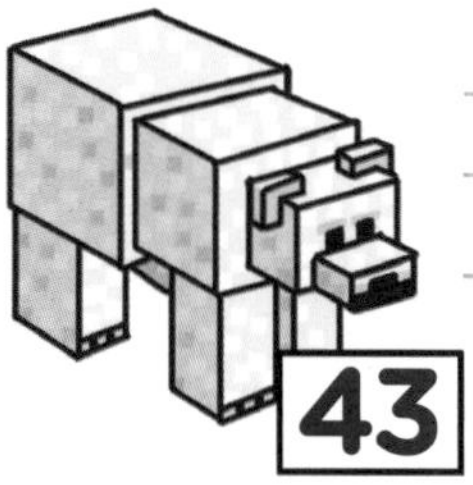

4.

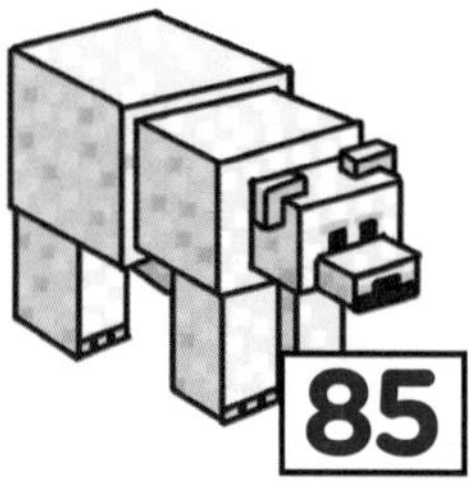

5.

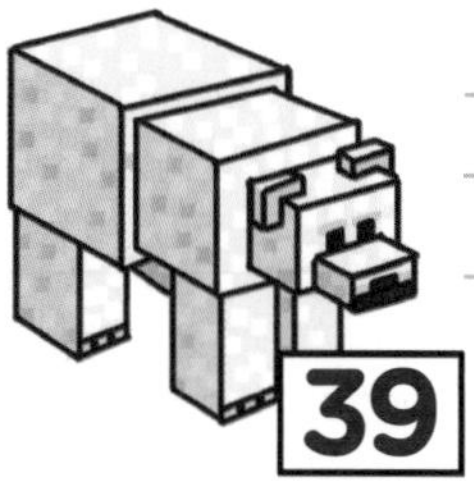

6.

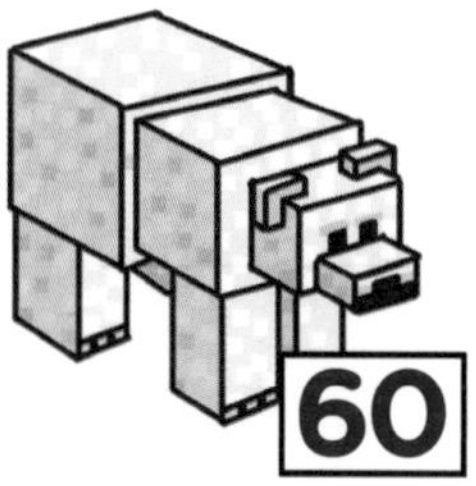

EXPANDED FORM IN BASE 10

Write the number on each ocelot in expanded form in the space provided.

Example:

$200 + 50 + 6$

256

1.

324

2.

849

3.

670

4.

506

5.

932

6.

481

ADDITION BY GROUPING

Circle the groups of 5. Then count on and write the total. The first one is done for you.

1.

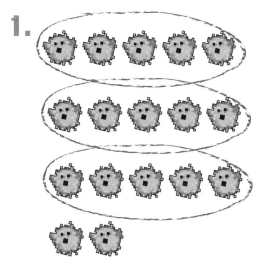

Answer: 17

2.

Answer: _____

3.

Answer: _____

4.

Answer: _____

5.

Answer: _____

6.

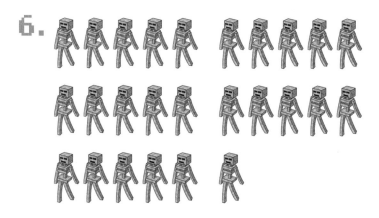

Answer: _____

MYSTERY MESSAGE
WITH ADDITION AND SUBTRACTION

Add or subtract. Then use the letters to fill in the blanks below and reveal the answer to Steve's joke.

1. $20 - 2 =$ _____ **S**

2. $14 + 3 =$ _____ **F**

3. $15 - 9 =$ _____ **A**

4. $6 + 13 =$ _____ **R**

5. $7 + 8 =$ _____ **E**

6. $13 - 6 =$ _____ **V**

7. $9 + 4 =$ _____ **L**

8. $18 - 6 =$ _____ **H**

Q: What do you call a silverfish that doesn't have any eyes?

Copy the letters from the answers above to solve the joke.

_____ _____ _____ _____ _____ _____ _____ _____ _____

6   18   13   7   15   19   17   18   12

SNOW GOLEM'S GUIDE TO PLACE VALUE

Write the number on the snow golem that matches the place value in the chart. The first one is done for you.

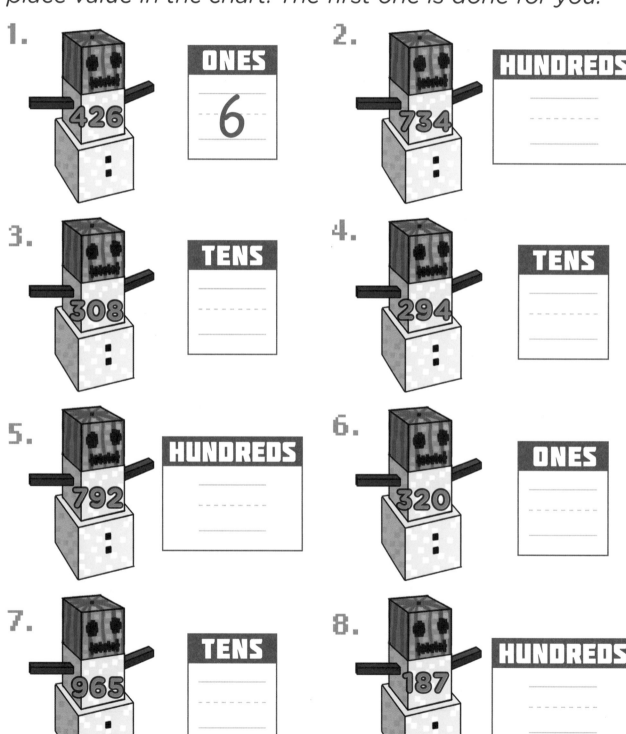

1. 426

ONES

6

2. 734

HUNDREDS

3. 308

TENS

4. 294

TENS

5. 792

HUNDREDS

6. 320

ONES

7. 965

TENS

8. 187

HUNDREDS

SKIP COUNT CHALLENGE

Count by 7s and fill in the empty spaces to help the witch get to the witch's hut.

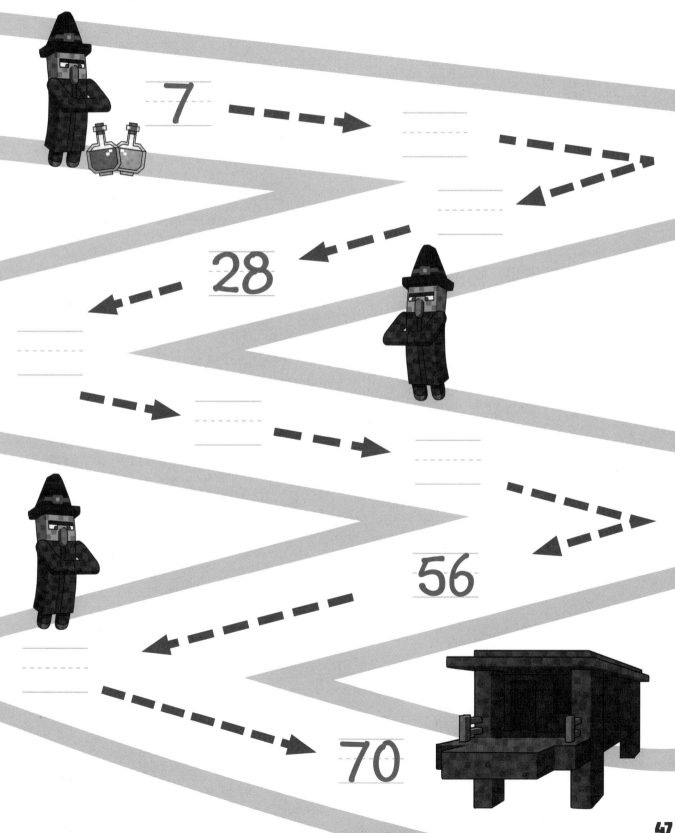

7

28

56

70

SUBTRACTION MYSTERY NUMBER

There is a number hidden behind these purpur blocks. Subtract to find the mystery number.

1.

$$18$$
$$- \ \blacksquare$$
$$2$$

$\blacksquare$ = _____

2.

$$16$$
$$- \ \blacksquare$$
$$6$$

$\blacksquare$ = _____

3.

$$20$$
$$- \ \blacksquare$$
$$7$$

$\blacksquare$ = _____

4.

$$15$$
$$- \ \blacksquare$$
$$15$$

$\blacksquare$ = _____

5.

$$16$$
$$- \ \blacksquare$$
$$2$$

$\blacksquare$ = _____

6.

$$20$$
$$- \ \blacksquare$$
$$3$$

$\blacksquare$ = _____

7.

$$12$$
$$- \ \blacksquare$$
$$1$$

$\blacksquare$ = _____

8.

$$19$$
$$- \ \blacksquare$$
$$0$$

$\blacksquare$ = _____

9.

$$18$$
$$- \ \blacksquare$$
$$6$$

$\blacksquare$ = _____

MYSTERY MESSAGE WITH SUBTRACTION

Add the answers from page 48 to the chart. Then use the chart to solve the riddle.

QUESTION	ANSWER	LETTER
1.		N
2.		A
3.		E
4.		T
5.		M
6.		I
7.		R
8.		H
9.		G

Q: What do you call a Minecraft horse wandering after dark?

Copy the letters from the chart to solve the riddle.

10 16 17 12 19 0 -

14 10 11 13

ADDITION IN BASE 10

Add the numbers. Then draw a line to the box with the correct place value. The first one is done for you.

1. 34 + 12 = 46

2. 17 + 12 = _____

3. 21 + 54 = _____

4. 17 + 71 = _____

5. 25 + 32 = _____

6. 11 + 51 = _____

7. 10 + 4 = _____

8. 31 + 6 = _____

ONES
8

TENS
5

TENS
4

ONES
2

TENS
7

ONES
9

TENS
3

ONES
4

SUBTRACTION IN BASE 10

Subtract the numbers. Then draw a line to the box with the correct place value. The first one is done for you.

1. 36 - 12 = **24**

2. 54 - 24 = ____

3. 67 - 25 = ____

4. 73 - 61 = ____

5. 87 - 21 = ____

6. 69 - 12 = ____

7. 99 - 18 = ____

8. 59 - 20 = ____

ONES
6

TENS
3

TENS
8

ONES
4

TENS
4

ONES
7

TENS
1

ONES
9

ADDITION MATH FACTS WITH 6 AND 7

Add the numbers.

1. 1 + 6 = _____

2. 1 + 7 = _____

3. 2 + 6 = _____

4. 2 + 7 = _____

5. 3 + 6 = _____

6. 3 + 7 = _____

7. 4 + 6 = _____

8. 4 + 7 = _____

9. 5 + 6 = _____

10. 5 + 7 = _____

11. 6 + 6 = _____

12. 6 + 7 = _____

13. 7 + 6 = _____

14. 7 + 7 = _____

15. 8 + 6 = _____

16. 8 + 7 = _____

17. 9 + 6 = _____

18. 9 + 7 = _____

19. 10 + 6 = _____

20. 10 + 7 = _____

MYSTERY MESSAGE
WITH ADDITION AND SUBTRACTION

Add or subtract. Then use the letters to fill in the blanks below and reveal the answer to Alex's joke.

1. $13 - 2 =$ _____ **M**

2. $4 + 16 =$ _____ **A**

3. $15 - 7 =$ _____ **S**

4. $6 + 13 =$ _____ **R**

5. $17 - 7 =$ _____ **W**

6. $13 - 8 =$ _____ **I**

7. $12 + 3 =$ _____ **O**

8. $16 - 9 =$ _____ **D**

Q: I'm very sharp and I'm always making a point. What am I?

Copy the letters from the answers above to solve the joke.

_____ _____ _____ _____
5   20   11   20

_____ _____ _____ _____ _____
8   10   15   19   7

ADDITION AND SUBTRACTION MATH FACTS 1-20

Add or subtract to find the answers.

1. 9 + 2 = _____

2. 8 + 3 = _____

3. 17 - 9 = _____

4. 16 - 5 = _____

5. 9 + 7 = _____

6. 12 - 5 = _____

7. 5 + 7 = _____

8. 9 + 9 = _____

9. 12 - 4 = _____

10. 7 + 7 = _____

11. 5 + 9 = _____

12. 16 - 8 = _____

13. 7 + 6 = _____

14. 8 + 4 = _____

15. 14 - 8 = _____

16. 4 + 7 = _____

17. 12 - 9 = _____

18. 4 + 9 = _____

19. 15 - 7 = _____

20. 7 + 8 = _____

SKIP COUNT CHALLENGE

Count by 8s and fill in the empty spaces to help Alex reach the End portal.

8

32

64

80

WORD PROBLEMS WITH ADDITION

Read the word problems. Use addition to find the answer. The first one is done for you.

1. You mine 3 iron ore blocks, 1 diamond ore block, and 5 granite blocks. How many blocks do you mine in all?

$$3 + 1 + 5 = 9$$

Answer: _9 blocks_

2. Alex crafts 2 gold swords at her craft table. The next day, she crafts 4 iron swords. The next day, she crafts 6 diamond swords. How many swords does Alex make?

___ + ___ + ___ = ___

Answer: _____

3. In his garden, Steve grows 7 carrots, 2 melons, and 6 potatoes. How many crops does Steve grow?

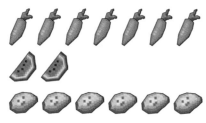

___ + ___ + ___ = ___

Answer: _____

4. Alex battles 5 ghasts, 3 skeletons, and 8 iron golems. How many mobs does Alex battle?

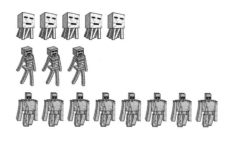

___ + ___ + ___ = ___

Answer: _____

WORD PROBLEMS WITH SUBTRACTION

Read the word problems. Use subtraction to find the answer. The first one is done for you.

1. The librarian has 20 books in the library. Alex borrows 5 books and Steve borrows 3 books. How many books are left?

$$20 - 5 - 3 = 12$$

Answer: _12 blocks_

2. There are 18 fish in the lake. Steve catches 4 fish one day and 3 fish the next day. How many fish are left in the lake?

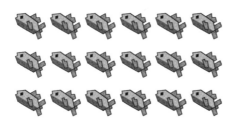

_____ - _____ = _____

Answer: _____

3. Alex sees 15 ocelots in the jungle biome. She tames 7 ocelots and Steve tames 5 ocelots. How many untamed ocelots are left?

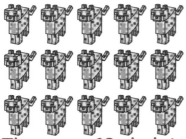

_____ - _____ = _____

Answer: _____

4. There are 12 skeletons. Alex destroys 2 skeletons and Steve destroys 4 skeletons. How many skeletons are left?

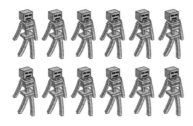

_____ - _____ = _____

Answer: _____

ADDITION AND PLACE VALUE

Add the numbers. Then write the values in the boxes. The first one is done for you.

1. $6 + 7 =$ 13

Tens	Ones
1	3

2. $8 + 4 =$ _____

Tens	Ones

3. $9 + 6 =$ _____

Tens	Ones

4. $16 + 4 =$ _____

Tens	Ones

5. $8 + 8 =$ _____

Tens	Ones

6. $12 + 8 =$ _____

Tens	Ones

SUBTRACTION AND PLACE VALUE

Subtract the numbers. Then write the values in the boxes. The first one is done for you.

1. 20 - 13=   7

Tens	Ones
0	7

2. 17 - 11 =

Tens	Ones

3. 19 - 9 =

Tens	Ones

4. 15 - 10 =

Tens	Ones

5. 20 - 7 =

Tens	Ones

6. 14 - 5 =

Tens	Ones

ANSWER KEY

Page 4

1. 5
2. 3
3. 6
4. 9
5. 4

Page 5

1. 8
2. 7
3. 5
4. 10
5. 14
6. 4
7. 12
8. 3
9. 15

Minecraft

Page 6

1. 5
2. 5
3. 7
4. 5
5. 8
6. 7
7. 7
8. 8
9. 10
10. 10

Page 7

2, 4, 6, 8, 10, 12, 14, 16, 18, 20

Page 8

1. 2
2. 5
3. 2
4. 3
5. 0
6. 4

Page 9

1. 2
2. 3
3. 2
4. 3
5. 4
6. 1

Page 10

1. 4, IIII
2. 7, ＷＷ II
3. 6, ＷＷ I
4. 5, ＷＷ
5. 3, III
6. 8, ＷＷ III

Page 11

1. 3, III
2. 4, IIII
3. 5, ＷＷ
4. 1, I
5. 6, ＷＷ I
6. 7, ＷＷ II

Page 12

1. 7
2. 9
3. 10
4. 5
5. 8
6. 4

Page 13

1. 5
2. 7
3. 3
4. 9
5. 8
6. 1
7. 6
8. 2

A skeleton

Page 14

1. 5
2. 3
3. 5
4. 6
5. 1
6. 0
7. 4
8. 9

Page 15

3, 6, 9, 12, 15, 18, 21, 24, 27, 30

Page 16

1. 3
2. 6
3. 5
4. 0
5. 4
6. 7
7. 8
8. 6

Page 17

Creeper egg

Page 18

1. 10
2. 10
3. 10
4. 10
5. 10
6. 10
7. 10
8. 10
9. 10
10. 10

Page 19

1. 2
2. 4
3. 3
4. 5
5. 7
6. 6
7. 9
8. 10
9. 1
10. 8

Page 20

1. 1
2. 2
3. 2
4. 3
5. 3
6. 4
7. 4
8. 5
9. 5
10. 6
11. 6
12. 7
13. 7
14. 8
15. 8
16. 9
17. 9
18. 10
19. 10
20. 11

Page 21

1. 3
2. 4
3. 4
4. 5
5. 5
6. 6
7. 6
8. 7
9. 7
10. 8
11. 8
12. 9
13. 9
14. 10
15. 10
16. 9
17. 7
18. 7
19. 2
20. 3

Page 22

1. 2 tens, 7 ones
2. 1 ten, 6 ones
3. 4 tens, 6 ones
4. 0 tens, 8 ones
5. 6 tens, 2 ones
6. 8 tens, 0 ones

Page 23

4, 8, 12, 16, 20, 24, 28, 32, 36, 40

Page 24

1. 4 wooden planks
2. 7 iron swords
3. 8 carrots
4. 6 melons

Page 25

1. 5 diamond blocks
2. 5 TNT blocks
3. 2 eggs
4. 5 wooden swords

Page 26

1. 6
2. 7
3. 9
4. 5
5. 9
6. 10
7. 7
8. 8

When you add an even number to an even number, the answer is even.

When you add an even number to an odd number, the answer is odd.

Page 27

1. 6
2. 4
3. 7
4. 3
5. 4
6. 1
7. 5
8. 2

When you subtract an even number from an even number, the answer is even.

When you subtract an even number from an odd number, the answer is odd.

Page 28
1. 5
2. 6
3. 6
4. 7
5. 7
6. 8
7. 8
8. 9
9. 9
10. 10
11. 10
12. 11
13. 11
14. 12
15. 12
16. 13
17. 13
18. 14
19. 14
20. 15

Page 29
1. 3 + 4 = 7
   4+3 = 7
2. 5 + 3 = 8
   3 + 5 = 8
3. 7 + 2 = 9
   2 + 7 = 9
4. 8 + 1 = 9
   1 + 8 = 9
5. 4 + 5 = 9
   5 + 4 = 9
6. 10 + 0 = 10
   0 + 10 = 10

The answers in each pair are the same no matter which number comes first.

Page 30
1. 9
2. 8
3. 5
4. 0
5. 2
6. 0
7. 6
8. 3

Page 31
5, 10, 15, 20, 25, 30, 35, 40, 45, 50

Page 32
1. 7 diamond blocks
2. 11 torches
3. 10 plants
4. 12 red mushrooms

Page 33
1. 3 tools
2. 5 plants
3. 8 horses
4. 7 pumpkin pies

Page 34
1. 15; 1 ten 5 ones
2. 12; 1 ten, 2 ones
3. 14; 1 ten, 4 ones
4. 20; 2 tens, 0 ones
5. 13; 1 ten, 3 ones
6. 20; 2 tens, 0 ones

Page 35
1. 9; 0 tens, 9 ones
2. 6; 0 tens, 6 ones
3. 10; 1 ten, 0 ones
4. 7; 0 tens, 7 ones
5. 16; 1 ten, 6 ones
6. 0; 0 tens, 0 ones

Page 36
1. 8
2. 4
3. 4
4. 3
5. 0
6. 6
7. 4
8. 7
9. 3
10. 1
11. 5
12. 5
13. 2
14. 5
15. 4
16. 2
17. 7
18. 3
19. 5
20. 2

Page 37
1. 6
2. 3
3. 5
4. 3
5. 1
6. 8
7. 4
8. 2
9. 7
10. 3
11. 3
12. 8
13. 4
14. 2
15. 4
16. 4
17. 6
18. 8
19. 4
20. 5

Page 38
1. 6 hundreds,
   2 tens, 9 ones
2. 7 hundreds,
   0 tens, 8 ones
3. 3 hundred,
   1 tens, 9 ones
4. 8 hundreds,
   3 tens, 0 ones
5. 9 hundreds,
   8 tens, 5 ones
6. 3 hundreds,
   0 tens, 4 ones

Page 39
6, 12, 18, 24, 30,
36, 42, 48, 54, 60

Page 40
1. 5
2. 7
3. 8
4. 10
5. 14
6. 6
7. 6
8. 15
9. 9

Page 41
Killer Bunny

Page 42
1. 90 + 1
2. 70 + 6
3. 40 + 3
4. 80 + 5
5. 30 + 9
6. 60 + 0

Page 43
1. 300 + 20 + 4
2. 800 + 40 + 9
3. 600 + 70 + 0
4. 500 + 00 + 6
5. 900 + 30 + 2
6. 400 + 80 + 1

Page 44
1. 17
2. 34
3. 7
4. 23
5. 13
6. 26

Page 45
1. 18
2. 17
3. 6
4. 19
5. 15
6. 7
7. 13
8. 12

A slverfsh

Page 46
1. 6
2. 7
3. 0
4. 9
5. 7
6. 0
7. 6
8. 1

Page 47
7, 14, 21, 28, 35,
42, 49, 56, 63, 70

Page 48
1. 16
2. 10
3. 13
4. 0
5. 14
6. 17
7. 11
8. 19
9. 12

Page 49
A night-mare

Page 50
1. 46
2. 29
3. 75
4. 88
5. 57
6. 62
7. 14
8. 37

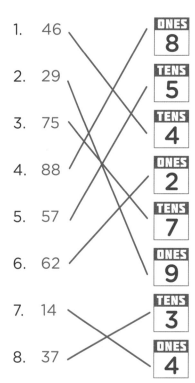

Page 51
1. 24
2. 30
3. 42
4. 12
5. 66
6. 57
7. 81
8. 39

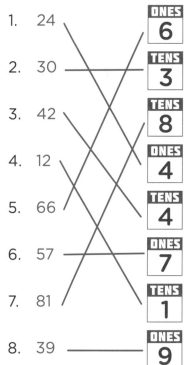

Page 52

1. 7
2. 8
3. 8
4. 9
5. 9
6. 10
7. 10
8. 11
9. 11
10. 12
11. 12
12. 13
13. 13
14. 14
15. 14
16. 15
17. 15
18. 16
19. 16
20. 17

Page 53

1. 11
2. 20
3. 8
4. 19
5. 10
6. 5
7. 15
8. 7

I am a sword

Page 54

1. 11
2. 11
3. 8
4. 11
5. 16
6. 7
7. 12
8. 18
9. 8
10. 14
11. 14
12. 8
13. 13
14. 12
15. 6
16. 11
17. 3
18. 13
19. 8
20. 15

Page 55

8, 16, 24, 32, 40, 48, 56, 64, 72, 80

Page 56

1. 9 blocks
2. 12 swords
3. 15 crops
4. 16 mobs

Page 57

1. 12 blocks
2. 11 fish
3. 3 ocelots
4. 6 skeletons

Page 58

1. 13; 1 ten, 3 ones
2. 12; 1 ten, 2 ones
3. 15; 1 ten, 5 ones
4. 20; 2 tens, 0 ones
5. 16; 1 ten, 6 ones
6. 20; 2 tens, 0 ones

Page 59

1. 7; 0 tens, 7 ones
2. 6; 0 tens, 6 ones
3. 10; 1 tens, 0 ones
4. 5; 0 tens, 5 ones
5. 13; 1 tens, 3 ones
6. 9; 0 tens, 9 ones